the
PITCH

Also by Tom Thompson

Live Feed

the PITCH

Tom Thompson

ALICE JAMES BOOKS
FARMINGTON, MAINE

10 9 8 7 6 5 4 3 2 1

Alice James Books are published by Alice James Poetry Cooperative, Inc.,
an affiliate of the University of Maine at Farmington.

Alice James Books
238 Main Street
Farmington, ME 04938

www.alicejamesbooks.org

Library of Congress Cataloging-in-Publication Data

Thompson, Tom.
 The pitch / by Tom Thompson.
   p. cm.
 ISBN-13: 978-1-882295-56-2 (pbk.)
 ISBN-10: 1-882295-56-0 (pbk.)
 1. New York (N.Y.)—Poetry. I. Title.

PS3620.H69P58 2006
811'.6—dc22

                          2005034557

Alice James Book gratefully acknowledges support from the University
of Maine at Farmington and the National Endowment for the Arts. ❧

Art ©Emilie Clark, 1999. Detail of untitled print, gouache, and graphite.
Collection of the author.

FOR MIRANDA

FOR WILLIE

FOR FINNIAN

Contents

Acknowledgements

For the friendship, insight and argument that helped bring these poems around, thanks to Miranda Field, Anthony McCann, April Ossmann, Sam Truitt, Sam Witt and Jon Woodward. And to the editors of the following journals for making space for these things to grow:

Boomerang: "Kitchenette," "Maquillage et Histoire" and "Red Light. Green Light." (all under different titles)

Boston Review: "You and Me"

Conduit: "Duenna" and "Observation Deck" (as "Monsieur B.")

Colorado Review: "After Cheese and Coffee," "The Goods" (as "Leather Goods"), "Scents of the Homelands" and "Shh, Now"

Columbia: "In Which I Find Myself Cast in a Dark Wood" and "Collect" (as "Slipstream")

Electronic Poetry Review: "A Promising" and "Votive Statuary" (as part of a larger poem, "The Virgin's Got Her Bachelors, Even"), "Copse and Robbers" (as "Mode et Accessoires Femmes") and "Tweezers Free a Look"

Kiosk: "Alba Bourgeois Tells Not a Soul" and "We Know More of You Outright Than We Can under Hypnosis Communicate (My Observers)"

The Hat: "A Fillip. A Fandango." and "Au Bar"

Volt: "A Seasonal Display," "Your Form Is Magnified by Dust" and "Landscape Drunk with You" (as "Post-Drunk Theory")

Xantippe: "Commute" and "Mode et Accessoires" (both as "Mode et Accessoires Femmes")

My translation of Baudelaire's *Paris Spleen* poem, "La Chambre Double" (which appeared in *Boomerang*) decomposed only to rematerialize in bits as "The Goods," "Classic Six," "Observation Deck" and "Your Own Finite Toes above a Small Tin Bath." "The Pitch" and "A Handsome Elevation" similarly grew out of my version of Baudelaire's "Invitation au Voyage," as did "Leashed, Lead" out of my version of his "Les Fenêtres." "Alba Bourgeois Tells Not a Soul" and "I Had an Idea, Was the New Guy" are for my friends in spam. "You and Me" is a mash-up of words and sentences from Hejinean's "The Fatalist," Emerson's journals and Da Vinci's notebooks.

The form of a city changes faster, alas!, than the heart of a mortal.
— CHARLES BAUDELAIRE

The Building with Glass Angled This Way and That

In from the street, inside folds, ascending
past glass walls swamped with sweat, fresh
plaster cold with lavender musk,
an inkling fragrance slips along
ropes and cables, feathers the edges
of this scaffold slapped together
high about the entryway, slips through
stairwells that shift blue luminescence into dark
as dreams shift waking, past
pinkish tissue in common spaces,
through rooms packed with anonymous
pockets, loose buckles, a weave
of machines wracked and frantic,
through an amazement of corner offices,
on past back cells, past
calculators, metronomes, pro-
gression, pacing, past
cost, price, bicker, patter,
billow-into-sale, past a woman
tense at a floor-to-ceiling window,
a man rigged to a shinier
situation, past the silk evidence
of sexual dismissals, the plastic
brink of broken celebrations, crepuscular
privacy curtains bolted to an iron frame,
past after past cast like ropes across
fault lines we dreamt or outlived
behind the tower's ruffled
frontage, this slung atmosphere
clinging to the windows all
particle driven and prickly about it.

The Pitch (Invitation au Voyage)

What superb rooms these are! A forest of chiffon and chifferobes,
quality divans you can exercise or dream upon.
Could we install ourselves here someday if we just hope for it?

It's a clouds-of-tulle kind of land this floating here
this blind milky liquor of Yankee fog.

Who sets up residence in this place sets up departure,
a don't-look-down kind of buoyancy. Angled out
at an imperceptible degree, the viewing portion suspends

sight on ringlets of steam so lush and glistening, tranquil and tensile,
that you don't notice your own toes down there somewhere,
weaving themselves into the carpet, enmeshed, mangled with pleasure.

It's absence masquerading as engulfment,

a hollow Mardi Gras head to plant your treacherous feet upon,
positioned pitch you use to negotiate sky, our spotless terrarium.

Taut grapes, sandwiches slathered pink
with meat and its fatty latticework, let these emphasize
the ever-ready beauty a stomach entails, its copious
and quickening. They form you out of immortal droplets,
my sweet-tongued blue, my ever prayed-for hunger.

Divider, chaos, dividend of the unforeseen—
these are your cold, erogenous fists.

Call it scrubbed verdigris or a meadow
mowed down like an army: it generates that kind of heat,

rises up the chart marked "Fantasy" with a bullet. So darkling,
you can put that nostalgia right in the bank.

See how this view enacts you? Everything impending,
as I said, where vision ladles a wicked pastoral
across the conference table, where deals are swapped
with delicate packets of parakeet breath,
where the silence between contraries is infused
entirely with pleasure. This is where you have to go, hunger,
the stretch you need in order to breathe, dream, cast hours
out to their infancy, where time pleads
no contest to pure sensation.

Here is your plushest countermand, the sister you choose and
    choose again.

And choosing, choose more so. It's hers, of course,
this fizz that grazes the good life, grisaille hours that curl,
styling the most thought thought,
her clock that bells absence like a cat.

And these gleaming panels. Filigreed. Sublimely lively sieves
you can use to modulate flow-through.
They're both calm and fantastical, hm?
As is the process that made them. The sunset's on automatic—
keeps re-jiggering the wall, trying to infuse
our apartments with glory—while ceiling tiles
sift roomfuls of grainy matter, satin beams
stutter through well-wrought window guards,
through lenses that divide us into numbered sections.

Mirrors, metals, goods of all kinds, silver nettles
woven round our necks by expert jewelers,
mammalian pottery fabulated in our image

by the most practiced craftsmen—all this
plays a silent symphony about our eyes. All these angles,
the cracks in drawers, pleats in drapery—
emit a singular scent, a manacled come-hither,
which is like the soul of the building itself.

This is the real estate of milk and honey, as I've said,
effulgent and rarefied transactions, brilliantine.
Consciousness glitters right along with the copper cookware,
ornate silverware, all the utensils mottled with age
and inestimable worth. These are the treasures
of the effable world, smack in the middle of this, what?—
perfume dealership—where one young clerk works another
as I work you and you me, a sweet frisson
that earns each of us to date, roughly,
the entire world in back pay.

After Cheese and Coffee

Sheets of copper and tin coated in a powdery glow. Roof gardens
blown open stem by stuffed-musket-stem below.

The daymoon plumps like melon. Even furniture
falls to its knees in this eclipse. Stretched forth, prostrate to
    shadow.

Your sturdy museum piece creaks in place,
gone all floral in waking dreamlight.

It takes on the mineral life of sleep, puts its soft,
vegetal tongue on display. It's a true flower's,
this tongue—*lick it*—

as the firmament is. The plush one

pressed to a wall

by laps swum, by every shunted sun.

Au Bar

Blue watts extend bar glass, tinting it, tilting—even this high up,
elsewhere extends itself in greeting across

                     a brass plate's selective surfacing.

Curved reflections catch

                     a crude velvet-topped stool,
its crippled circling, circling

                     in the corner, this

frittering furniture we set our asses to. So many entrances
beauty scuffs against.

                 There's a loose cable,
                    electrified, dripping ivy.

A sweet, fat notion of sun pulses outside—
survival or eternity or making it—

where rooftops stretch for decades below us.

All Scents Rise

They draw you at a remove, these

                              cashmere rooms,

slip you up on a wire of want

through corridors swarmed with childhood prayers,

                                  pressing intimations

of past and present, a slew of options that house

and assume your form

                                      as waters do,

                    container swelling

to contained—a building not so much above the clouds as of

                    the clouds, bundling

tight to the glass.

                                Where work crews

worry their safety lines outside, a sudden drop

casts up

                    wisps where they were—

                        forty stories high and counting.

A Handsome Elevation

Such incomparable apartments, superior to all others, as Art is to
   Nature,
where matter emulates apparition,

where all is sudden, corrigible, embellished, completely remade.
Failed alchemists of sediment and flower

who tug back and back, pulling forever at the edges of their
   happiness,
keep working at that frantic garden, that zero-sum sunset.

Incomparable embudment. Forced tulip as fragile as math,
it's here you're meant to unfold, somewhere in this play of
   correlation.

The more spacious and tactile a soul grows, the more sleep tugs at
   the possible.
This is the scene you recall from that breathing screen

where your own brief rumor was caught
minutes or months ago, that scene you so uncannily resemble.

These techniques, this furniture, the bird-like order and perfume,
   such meticulous organisms,
they're you and you again—

vast, curious, alien to the touch, armed with hidden depths and
   surface locks,
these most social and hostile refinements.

Enormous rivers and mellifluous canals are slung through the
    land-sheen before us.
Endless cargo trucks bearing endless goods,

brimming with necessities, rising and falling on the monotonous
    waves of radio work songs.
These are the routes set by sleep's paving stones, smoothing end-
    lessly over your remains—

they ease you toward glass. We call that Infinity,
as harbor light pools the uppermost atmospheres;

as clarity and volume of space is measured by the twinkling of
    landing gear, rising;
as these ships of yours return to their native ports—exhausted by
    the swells,

engorged on the unreachable. They swing the riches back around
as if it's you who approaches, you who receives.

Eau de Nile

Who's gold? The dome down there is not for prayer
though the curve of it suggests your au contraire—
snuggles tight in your sleep and vanishes come morning.

☾

You shred trails nightly—payrolls, practicum, the pretty
leads that string you along. It's why you got that frantic machine,
produce fine confetti for citywide celebrations. It's empty now,

☾

the street, an eau de nile poured out in sticky runnels,
crystalline splinters, sparklers ground into the avenue,
where foot traffic came and went and went.

☾

We Know More of You Outright Than We Can under Hypnosis Communicate (My Observers)

Methods to produce an infinite number of ourselves are encoded
in the streets' laying-down process. More than method,
my Own, my Personal, you should know that these are the fiats,
precious ones, coalescing under my passing feet. The glamour glass
has long since passed shard by shard to asphalt-black and back again
using flesh, using rubber, a length of bone, a picture of Mother.
These are the trinket tokens, lip gloss warming a three-year-old boy,
pencil shavings gathering at the fingertips as a sign (if you'd like one).
You keep me from passing through by shifts in radio frequency,
don't you, darling. Shifts in air—how it slaps at the knees
with bits of paper, cigarette stubs, parts of my own distinctive pigeon.

"Dear will-a-way," you say to me, "you fare badly in crowds:
putting your tongue to the ground, batting the small child in the back"
(he makes that hollow "Oh" sound,

it comforts us). Reared by anxious-wolves-
all-in-white, I've grown addled by the late park's part and glow,
its minute-to-minute blush, ambivalent heed,
ambergris feel, how it cuts off each thread of design
before it can be applied.
Must we be so conscious at every stage of our passing?

Streetlight flows in the head and out the hide. I offer you, fair
observers, fistfuls of flesh-colored band-aids to help staunch the tide,
and some more transparent. I have the underwear
in shrink-wrapped packets, cans of gasoline and corn,
enough paperclips to melt into one hell of a bullet: provisions
to withstand the muted agitation and terror of national councils,
the era of someone else's revolution.

All about us, lost friends drift in last season's evening dress—
sinister instances of body fluids passing from actual events into an
    excruciating,
exclusive dormancy we're not to know about, just spread.
But what happens when knowledge exceeds our capacity to act?

No observer is permitted to know any other observer,
though none could exist without the sum total. Some can see
how at a certain ring-tone phantom notions take shape,
the way store fronts shudder awake with awnings that flutter
and snap against tin poles and lead air. The very streets
crackle and hum, and a scream of seeming delight
emerges from the manhole ten feet away.

Something's being fixed. Someone's being lost. All these
in this morning of that noontide—in all their protozoan aspects,
in the private dissuasions of interior laws ("How do you feel,"
doctors ask and then ignore). The sun grinds itself
down to a set of shiny keys, more or less fitting a series of locks,
slipped firmly into our howling pink and custom-built fists.

Observation Deck

Here, indisputably here: two blast-yellow
dawns that stretch   this sear of dusk.
Two slowly, speechlessly   mouthing compacts
in which you recognize beauty's   flat malice.
They swim, they cease,   they swallow
any gaze foolish enough   to approach them.
You've been studying them,   these blank stars.
They command attention   and admiration.
And what sweet device   should you become
in the face of this   teetering ambition?
Enraptured, entrained   by these coverings
and absences,   by new realms of catch and loss,
your most anxious ecstasy   is you. You
this figure referred to as life,   harkened to
like some stainless   booming expansion.
But contentment   has nothing in common
with this towering divinity   you know now,
that you lust after   minute to minute, second to second.
No. No more minutes!   No more seconds!
Progression's a wash.   The ticks, eternal itching
gewgaws. Hail your own   personal anonym,
that succulent creature   whose stalkish toes
are placed effortlessly   in your teeth.

The Goods

Strip these walls to the hide,   skin them of art, paper.
Compared to pure animal   to the unthought thought
beauty keeps trying   to cure you, string you up
by your most private functions.   Muslin you chose seasons ago
weeps effortlessly across   interior portals, pours
about your four-poster.   It's forever falling, abandoning itself
like snow. Horizon's surge,   its have-what-may.
Only the most precise endearments   point to continuing,
you must point to yourself.   Walls assume the texture
of sucked lozenge, a whiter than white   that rubs you
with the delicious clarity   of a bled thing.
Let room equal everything   not wall, it rings
with formless yet distinct harmonies: traveler's clock,
sugary girders listing   within concrete ideas,
street sweepers grinding up silence.   Sounds flatten
the city below to a meadow of seepage,   dissolving lattice.
The slightest breath   contains the whole of our volume.
Adrift in a colorless dawn   something wakes, startled
by the building's heat   closing in, cracking a knuckle,
tapping your shins   with its small *what* and shiny.

Your Own Finite Toes above a Small Tin Bath

The building's sleek airs hiss in the pipes, compressed
slow as rose, the rose slows to blue
spritzings of regret and
who-cares-for-it-anyway—out of the speckled valve
                              a dual-chambered action—
atomized to a fog of longing. *Monsieur,*
the slung spoor works for you, so use it. Never does quite
condense into a body, does it, the late gold
atmosphere. It grinds,
wet with indeterminate particles, cast-off
                              forms, pulverized cornerstones,
disjecta that cloak your membranes
                    like baby powder. Looks soft, anyway.
And makes for a uniform belief
you're likely to welcome over the two-fold breath,
the rose the blue the bubble and toil
                    of your daily lungs.

Doctored Emerson

Doctor, I'm a clever girl. Could you be my calling?
The capable tower withstands weather.
Our sweater-lock, worked up in grime, is charred only a little bit
where the Bic took hold of our fumbling thumbs. My gossamer
    hairline
got edged by a practical razor into rough strands.
Tell lies and your girlfriend will pass by,
Doctor. Watch me. Passing by.

Sugarcane liquor makes my breath thick and stowaway.
Skin's oxygenations seem tiny in comparison, tiny plastic hammers
applied to soft spots in the city's underpinnings.

Sparrows skitter-a-bob at the pale bits.
There's a breakthrough and my head skips off like a doll's—
only to become a citation in someone else's thesis.

One is always hungry here but all there is is pizza,
Doctor, Doctor, apple of my eye.

So you say, "That, too, is an elastic feeling." Say it in as natural
a flatness as any the countryside ever served up.

This city of mine lies down with eyes clamped shut, arms and legs
    rigged
stiff as lead pipes. Well, they are lead pipes with an arsenal's effluvia
passing through. Radios stutter purposefully while a cat sets off
a stray wall of animosity.

What was once our nation's cleanest water is now known
to be populated by agitating microbes, an invisible sin

when it passes certain lips. What you drink with
or without agreeing to, it kills you either way.

All rumors are beautiful, doctor. "Do your work
and I shall know you."
That's a good one. And these I've pressed on you
with both hands clapping, clapping, blowing you up in a glass.

Kitchenette

The wall peels back   to landlord white,
then the rosy hue   lateness leaves you to.
Grit trickles past   your shoe, alight
on air, but just.   You can't call this
arch furrow home.   Call it the rise
of illumination   or the fall of night,
sway governs here   either way.
You must choose   your face with care
and with abandon.   Pull back from
naked sightlines,   the neighbor building's
windows where eyes   or imperfections
blink back across the way.   The hands up close
yellow with vegetable age,   disease. "How I love
to scrape myself,"   the cars repeat, below.
How you adjust the mirror   in your kitchen.
The TV monitor's 8-inch half-light   flickers
unaccountably,   pixels widening like pores
into pure static. The sound   a static frippery
that worries at your skin,   minute fingernails,
an electrical insistence   on fall-lines and fasciculi.
The picture resumes   with a bride-to-be
bulging with patience,   her explosion into night.
Stay local then.   Refuse knowledge
and other reversible stances.   Tomorrow
keeps forgetting to exist,   and you? Brimmed
to bursting. Another   frayed electrical cord
spits and hums across the airshaft,   spritzing itself
with sparks.   You want weather to suit you,
provide a lush field   to slow movement's
moment in. Set this   field of change
against dusk's ever-erstwhile,   cultivate
such hushed eruptions   as dust is known by.

Classic Six

I spent years selecting this place,
and then forgot the reasoning that put me here.
Take this entrance hall, the precise space
I nominated for a personal future, that doubles

now as a cloak room. Take my aunt's furniture,
all cock-eyed and shameless, the faux fireplace
done over in gesso and frayed plasterboard,
the suite coated in amphibious naugehyde,

chandeliered in smashable solitude.
It's all mine, pre-fathomed, limed and irrigated.
That awful caulking that warps the sill
is my doing. And yet, such fine lines rain drools in the dust.

And the florid detritus of another world, that sensuous perfection
that sent me swooning? The fetid must a childhood dog gives off,
the shaggy mold of endlessness that permeates everything.
It ransacks you; it's in the lungs.

My precious files are stacked and molting by the bed,
scratched-out, riddled with errors of tone, the driest expressions
so much stiff lingerie to linger in, a collection of spidery signatures
that, page by page, give themselves off to air.

I've grown thick, pinched and fat with disuse,
diffuse fumes bunched up by concrete towers
into an enviable sunset. Painted red. Pointed to the wall.
Remember those ends of day back when we lived downwind?

It was country then
or went by its name. Is it I think or remember? Not both.

Mode et Accessoires

Chocolates on offer in the glass house—
they glisten

at the surface-to-surface
furnished by a passing act,

its horizontal nature. Glance along
a shoulder beneath

the dress's bunched tempests
of fabric, skin

blowsy with heat. A stray pulse—mine
or yours—dissolves.

In every action there are layers
of inaction, anonymity

as seamless as the sea. Beauty
eats at you. We call it

depth. It is horizon and endless style.

Alba Bourgeois Tells Not a Soul

Birth squeezes the body high and low,
wet, alone for authenticating purposes.

For an instant in the laughing night
Drew Jaramillo spoke to me

and speaking so became my triumph.
The heavens weigh on me, towering

too earthly to think on it.
The sourness of the present age

clamps down. There are some—
Felicia Leon is one—who use words like "wings."

Well, Felicia, I don't appreciate it.
The globe is spinning itself tighter and tighter,

until no hope for escape. Our rockets
have neither fuel nor form enough.

There's a bounty on our heads, posters
here and there with our pictures on them,

though we've done nothing…
Perhaps that's just it, if we had made some

thing, created some activity, we'd be free?
I might as well lie to myself now,

since even campfires are getting put out
with water cannons. All is not well, my immortal

Milo Tackett, and dying makes it worse.

Stoplights Are Gaping with Cold (My Observers)

The stoplights are gaping with cold, emitting finger shapes, streaky
    and thing-like.
They thrill to ground's flat guises as snow does, take a turn at
    ground's porous qualities,
flattening experience at the surface—as snow does.

        White weather trills
(its sonic guises) makes crazed patterns
of ice, a whozzat-patter   at ground level.

These patterns want for nothing. Don't speak of them.
Were we looking for a pure icon of the senses?
No, we were looking for you, Tom Thompson.
        False image composed of fresh motion.

            There, beyond reach,
that body attached to these eyes by colorless threads—
    woozy, wandering drunk
flattened against festive blocks of color, memory
in the person of that girlfriend who didn't care for you,
squeezing you, pinching under the arms, at the seams, your crotch.

How the cold embraces us! It beads light into sexed-up nubs,
    creates such a vibrant yet stationary audience.

    The stoplights are tethered to music. They tender us,
shoulders first, to the conditions of dance, sweating us, even as we
    aspire to pure metal. Menial. To cling as meniscus clings.

Asphalt grows silken in an effort to impress the lights but
    impresses us instead.
It hisses at snow and snow retreats, a kind of sibling behavior.

Likewise,
our vehicles answer each other—

cascade for cascade—a peristaltic rhythm, belting and snorting.

The cars are an embarrassment to the lights and their dreams
of self-sufficiency. They depend, hanging
on the hanging lights, whose plastic encroachments try us
                              at length, only to find us gone.

Votive Statuary in a Rooftop Garden

She's error's whipped peak, plasti-form,
impulse-bought.

Some *Thank you, Jesus*, some *regret*

to inform you
I can't get myself to relinquish. Her shoulders
half shrug, half take-it-back.

Slight fissures down her

side have been sealed over,
congealed with

coagulate. What is it

I have done again?
Feeling licks its claws too early to take bets.

Constellations of decay decorate the
wax-white gown—

spattered blood or shattered
insect bits, a loose trail, strewn evidence

of a snapped path
I've got half a mind to.

Maquillage et Histoire

Piled up along with our portables, eyeliner,
travel packs of ipecac—all that dust, drifting.
        It gets hot like this and the applicant pool dries up.
                Our flats slap down
and the street thrums back. Spent pellets

litter a market, GORE-TEX in your hem glitters forever.

There is no waste. There is no debt.
A thin powdery stream leaks from the flagship store—

        "ambrosial ash" or "piecemeal gravel"—

drives foot traffic into duelling data streams.
           Who's on point? The newscopter
     pulses, sharpens the air.

A Promising

A tendency, tired as I am, risen
as I am to this wind-shaken,
rooted boat of a building,
en haut and swaying at the point
you fail to kiss me.
A barking breaks out, fizzles
to a siren I attend without meaning
or prospect of. Steam
rattles the pipes, a caged thing
creasing the air between us.
It's emptied, pressed,
a wee bit torn but
ready to wear. Sun
bears down on my hinges
and as suddenly lifts,
airing me out,
lording me, twirling me up
like the real ballerina action
that rises out of your jewel box—
a ritual promising, a whorled plastic
specimen endlessly nestling
amid a low-ceilinged sky,
sparkling dustfields of charge
and play. Tens of tiny mirrors
riff off the willowy lamp,
my tissue and limbs, toss
poppies and poppies of light
at the window to melt into
here-no-here. Mouths
open what we put our mouths to.

Leashed, Lead

Ask each other in your sitting room, the look a kind of question
projected through the glass between you, stylish partition
                                        veined in gleam, framed
indications of how anxious she is.

Horded yes, shrouded as she is

in your own coal black outline as others are veiled
in God or grief. Nothing
richer, more mysterious, more depthless and inviting.
                                How drawn she looks, her

transparency shot through with the brilliant and binding,
                        panes streaked with weightlessness.

Solitary? Try shadow-sponge, amassed liquid.

Out in a full-on flash, my predicate, there's nothing as absorbing as
        you in this
lens between spaces—flicked off from your functions. A fervency
        for information
assumes the form of your own face, so life-like, which is to say

                                        alight

in this flat black trough, buzzing—cars somewhere down below
        staticky with the goods and the ongoing rush of the world
entire, rivering in endless adjustments.
                                It gapes back at you

this black pause of yours—shadow's

                                    molten seal, banked,

pendulous, pulled   weight on your tongue.

Duenna

A collar out of Fra Angelico   flickers across
the wall display—   modifiable bit by bit,

a cloaked form falls   to its knees in a room
in a far off city.   Is this a sexual film or a spiritual one

shadowing the wall?   It feels real under my finger-stubs,
humming.   By the window a spider-spindled ivy

is gowned in delicate dust,   extrudes patience from itself
leaf tip by leaf tip.   The greening tips sheathed in white

reach for a way out,   or in, through their own lit reflection.

Commute

October's evening gloves press your arms to lunar gelatin, silence
the elbows and bangles, the angular silver fruit...
                Leafmold at your ear, nearest. Beefy cold.

       O's blown prose dusts up anklets and pumps, skipping by
red handpulls, glancing off chrome floors, walls—the new train
look, air
          tight about your clutchbag, dearest—freeze there, clear.

"O," says I, as in "yoke" and "yolk."

Railcar's empty amphetamine
        but for you and me and me and me. Each strap-hold

quotes neck harness theory with one steel loop.
             You must recalibrate the ticklish compact
between powder and gold seasonally.

Ornament and Gauge

Ice huffs brief pearls across the lake. Sky's metallic luster
a bit recherché say the groundsmen.

Overruled.

Breath assumes a riderless shape, sparkling fear, all rise and catch in
    a tunnel of branches.

It's a troubling time drives flight craft mad with the living. The
    sound of watching
indistinguishable from the white noise that precedes it.

I get admitted to the upper world temporarily—

sustained ghost frittering in heat-sensitive cameras.

A Fillip. A Fandango.

The police set about their work so tenderly! Like dolls built to
    simulate laughter.
Like bells, they watch the space between themselves, not us. Its
    milky white.

Their whos and wherefores have been smudged for our enchant-
    ment. Once-upon-their-bodies
steamed good and stiff right into those ruffled blackcoats.

And that's how we like them, flushed, immobile to our bootless
    haste, to the loose cargo drifting by—
calliope of tin and cash, dashing asphalt.

We like each pistol's toy piano ping, how it signals adjustments
to temperature, alters by degrees our own satisfactions, pin by pin,

a sound to rejoice in, as the police rejoice, without moving
your lips or eyelids. The held sigh of a nebula, swelling.

How we envy the buckles that clasp back at them.
Their radios, looser, lean into the white air—thumbed post-
    coitally, mindful, yet distracted.

Their leather straps have been lathered and scraped and are
    lathered again by fog's fur-based intelligence,
that we wrap about our shoulders, that a splatter of ice-mud clings
    to, latched, raffiné with frost.

Gloss, Upwards

The water towers of New York are shivering like egg sacs.
Shall we tell them to get down from there?

Their hairy legs attract the wind
up where they were so recklessly scattered

by their mothers—those phosphorescent
and desperate to be shed of the past.

I fear our own contents are famed and not a little dangerous
to the water towers and their mossy drives.

Hear them whinge in the distance like tree tops?
It's the wet season and terrible to the towers.

Leaves rise up like the dead scratching to get in.
Dust motes grow by magnitudes of ten

until they clog each air hole and drainage spout,
strip all remnants of signage

with a black tar-like substance that works itself
between the slats and under the nail heads,

pushing in, displacing original materials
bit by bit until each tower is itself

a wholly owned subsidiary of leaves.
It's their despair at this process

that leads to the towers' dream of imploding

directly over our bedrooms,

drenching our night-things with a violent passivity.
It's here, when they think of us, that we have them.

So radiantly and anonymously do they prepare for us,
in such individual-size portions.

Their various livers are drained to a single lethal point.
Their lungs and allowances and private social codes,

all their ambulatory innards, become our own.
Burying us quite silently from the inside. The way we like it.

Scents of the Homelands

The window smells of someone   else's apples. Caw
comes from a raw tree,   its branches bare of everything
but the caw: A birdless sound   not quite hungry,
not quite not, occupies space   like an invisible army,
like the one buzzing in your breadbasket.   Leaves
swirl in a signature scribble.   Their swishes
swap nothing for air, make room   for low-flying jets
on your breakfast tray,   more sirens sliding shut
your throat.   Mind love's pitched scent for once,
trading targets with silence,   ignoring the sleep that flashes
blank chambers at you.   All night you spent cocked
with waking, shackled to copters   closing in and as
suddenly gone in the   calm-enough morning.

There's a Hugo Wolf in the Woods (My Observers)

Here you are my nail-thin boy, all angular fidgets beneath the big
    red car.
Stop fingering those solitary hairs. That's a shadow's job,
a dented ball's circling, circling the blow-up pool.
Against the fence, privacy grows antiqued by ivy, prickly, tense.
Linger, here, over this moveable zoo of gravel.

Nixed nightlong in moon-gown cotton
I synchronize my mouth with yours. Singsong
nonsense is one way to take your fear and feed it
to the baroque crows lining the phone wire.
Other methods prune mother's perfume back to a show of teeth.

And my fatherly hip? The jabbing spot where bone sticks out.
A bluish bouquet of inattention blooms around your mouth.
We've talked about this before, rewired your jaw especially....
A metallic trickle is fixed to the spout in our cast-iron pond.
How about a walk in the institute woods? Bodies slough off
a nervous distillation of thought eventually. They sink
into the ground, alluvial, alleviated. Even melancholy surrenders

its green zeal to the trees. They are its weakest point as they are
    mine.
If I could start over from a grassier point.... Some way to sashay
among the yards, bore keenly through each back fence
with steady astonishment. But slowness

is my revelation. It forms such holes as squirrels do.
To feed. To pass through. The yard's cracked
rain-streaked devotional statue weeps a tune
you have to speed up the tape to hear. It tears. How like

our neighbors to stand as amalgamated
prefects. The sun is still some
lopped one. It wants in, too. Leaves dither, unsure
whether to absorb or repel; so they do a little of both.

Copse and Robbers

In the swim of the pool, a scrim of algae snoods your hair,
fingers down your suit.
The surroundings want to indulge you. It's a form of belief,
their watching. Trees, too,
root through your things looking
for a weapon.

Rough Sketch for a Shinier Forest

Our plans, okay,
drawn on the very best material.
If it's not titanium, I'm not interested. Piston
the leaves up higher. Fashion new buildings
from smoke. Brushed, right? That's what we make of it.
Our needs are plenipotentiary
and forever in debt to the depletor.
A him? Ahem. Wispy god, indelicate
haze we only need some of in this mirrory city.

Red Light. Green Light.

The new sneakers feature   a billowing action,
ways to help feet track   new regimens of avoidance.
It's not working.   The leaves are too bright; they close
the sky off to all but sound.   The private jet mimics
a public bomb, asks   if you'd rather be a victim
of chance or intention.   The newsagent smiles in a way
you can't read. The subway grate   buckles and steams
with foot traffic,   crossings the mayor promotes
as "the new flight."   Not catching air, but outdistancing it.
Like these markers you use   to pace yourself—a banner
to duck, cabs that circle   your matador cloak, sludge
thick enough to skitter over.   Such vertical seclusion
opens you to the guard   who flinches as you slip
past his pause.   Readjust your featureless face.

I Had an Idea Was the New Guy

But not therefore out of touch. Perhaps therefore too in touch?
Sensitive to the not-me all around. Marjorie Harding,
for example. Carson Root. Esteban Flanagan.
I loved in the way loving is simply a swerve of want.

I signed up to give Isidro Sullivan his official party
but then the music started and Lindsey Grubbs wandered in
with her spangled vest looking for something real.
And there, indeed, we were. Had a great time, got drunk,
kissed some in the shadows with lips we called our own.

A Seasonal Display

Your avenue is hive and jewel, restive.
The after-thicket of bright exhaust

stiff where entrance swells
shoulder-bag-to-shoulder-bag with exit.

So "not me." So stand clear.
Your destination is implied, dear we.

There's always something else to see.
A brick. A bauble. A caught explosion.

Calfskin gloves carve
a track into soot and wall tiles

grown brackish, all grip and broach.
Quite a museum says the honey.

Quite a sticky. Customers string themselves
across storefronts glazed

with spray-on frost. Your eye sets
piecemeal, here

against the pliant, near-liquid pane—breath
tacks up slow blankets to muffle the glass.

Snow Longs for Balance

Snow's an animal for balance, drawn tight
to our building-tops, clutching
at the air conditioner's vibrato.
It neither fears nor glories in the winds that wrap it
across the East River, makes of the brown
scudding cream a dream of poured concrete.
The more snow layers itself over roofs and roads,
the more inner air it applies
to the outer, a transfer of heat so perfect,
an osmosis so complete, that motion itself
grows void. Such a threat to our carnal maneuverings!
Such a treat for our twin engines of doubt and sex.

Collect

Starlings bicker over
landfill, glints
about their wings and tin
clamor. Grist
long since settled
between spark and sequence.
You turn to runoff
to drink, the rumbling
under-girdings that
feed migration's slough.
The birds battle sleep
forever overhead,
carrying to it a
clang of *–ing* and *–ing*,
metallic echo chamber
called into being each time
you cry out
for what's fucked—the faulty
vessel, panicky
tissue, sheared, collapsed,
extracted this strict
way you hadn't remembered
to expect.

Tweezers Free a Look

My glance slips along finer and finer pairs of shoes,
        skipping up to a sky so pure it irritates the eye.
The rougher the wind the more spectacular

        its spangling of the windfence.
Nature's shout is too transparent
        in its throwing down its raising up

too obsessive a devotion to things of the world.
        Off a far roof the fall flash fall I can't stop
following. Even the small buildings

        fizz behind leaf shroud. And grackles,
cackling, the ringers and stunners, the gingham-clad,
        all these nervous squads ripple out between

maples, forming ragged strips of color,
        whipping cracked Maypoles, choking me
with *la da la di.* Trunks keep time

        a strict cadence while their branches
snip flounces of updraft and canopy,
        layering a sky within the sky,

one that finally pushes back.

Report on the Willows in a Time of Color

The willows that enjoy the fall are those that sleep
as a team of whippets sleep. They let wind like blood,
make succulence a succinct thing. Intricate now, as vascular
systems expertly flayed. These willows infer nothing
from the slack fevers gathering about their root systems—
feral drifts of grass, unmoored shadows of swans,
dream-like bodies guarding the willows' internal structure
loosely and with the odd crack of firearms.
Their skin has been applied by such lithe hands,
practiced in so exacting and delicate a violence,
that you cannot engage trees like these in conversation
nor distract them with tossed stones. They are not sad
so much as stringent, not doomed so much as enticing,
not eloquent themselves so much as a tool for surrender,
an amazement of brachia, prepared for the cry.

Your Form Is Magnified by Dust

Dusk approaches
with transmission wire in its hand.
Another bee
particular about its nectar.
Another bee with a tube down its throat.
Don't wilt on the demi-floor, me,
amassed amid motes
in memory's ever-antechamber.
A choking kind of laughter draws
my sense from the sorting room to the tarmac
back behind the cottage. Lines for garters.
Lines for phones. Lines of songs
mumbled to lull me by, pitched
under the canvas-black
where a body grows heavier,
forgetful. Sleep tugs
at matter, wincing where the live bit
pinches, the privet's raw cutaway.
Ignore the pistil,
it smells of sunspot and crash.
Ignore myself,
melting under the ants' finicky regimen.
There's sugar there at the tip
of each tongue. A gleam
in the petals palpitates, night's
pale button still sticks.

Shh, Now

The lake is tired of always playing the mother.
It gathers at the silt layer in tiny balls of algae.

It wants no more of your grief and the sheets
Of information you press on it. Really now,

Who swirled you into such impossible patterns
That a lake would surrender its claim to you?

The lake refuses you just as the birds refuse
The lake. White birds

With brittle feathers. Their beaks stuck shut.
It snarls around on itself, this lake,

To slather its balls—you understand me?
It has no use for us, closing its one

Historic eye before we ever get to use it.

In Which I Find Myself Cast in a Canopied Wood

We steer by call, wrong call
            or ricochet. So when
radiance comes we go

            with it even if it blinds us.
Wood gone. Dark gone.
            Dashed asphalt churned

to memory, then metaphor,
            now useless. We fed
our sight so greedily

            on so many forms—those
hip-tight and corseted,
            stuffed, cut and stitched—

that even after they left
            scraps remained, dried
into fall leaves, overspill

            of clinked glasses, grasses
that rise from rust.
            Sun reveals itself

mere scold in the ways
            it makes eyes, takes off.
Not even singular. Not even wave.

            We're stuck to these
stabs at seeing, at stars
            that multiply like sequins,

blowing the constellations out
                whiter than white until they become
useless for telling the way.

                Let's mark time
then, domestic animal.
                Consider détente

with each wall
                of light, refuse it.
This back and forth,

                you know, is what made
the named beasts ample.
                Not us.

The Benches

In this mountain air we achieve
without benefit of any actual mountains,
you can train your body
according to the exacting principles
of your own distinctive pleasure—
she says—if that's what you want
here on this cold stone bench
wet with November's outtakes.

Esprit d'Escalier (My Observers)

Clatter in the hall announces me here at your stranger door. Faced with this amazement of locks, I lay my knuckles thick upon it until your fingers tunnel through powdery stops, slide bolts back and forth. Tap and rattle at the spy hole like change in a pocket. None of it's exact. Measure pleasures itself by internal means: a tender pane, a moist and fickle syringe. Something layered and hairy about us, in the fallopian manner, fiddles with what passes through, flushed with having to pull the costume on this early. However fitting or ill-fitting an age, it's still strewn silk and horsehair. Reports are finding these human environs less and less credible. Sitting for a new sound could help, a bit of methane in the bedroom maybe, maybe re-hang the cabinet, anything to fend off bed and its nightly hang-ups, hooks at your back, silver where the whirring went.

Bubbles

Baubles. No,
bubbles busy at the surface, then a single
lead-color circle creeps by degrees
out. Not round, but oval
like your freelance eye, expert
and inexact. Pull back the ceiling lamp
to expand the entrance pool,
trigger the moon you arch, half-gothic,
over to see—where clouds
emerge in the water, hover, fine wisps
and fluids that form a machine
made of plasma, flimsy defense
for idle hands. A lone touch at the rim
scatters the clean display
in ripples. And now
you thread sparkling white pebbles
into an unmade bed. Mussed
and strange to itself,
the brain-crowd fidgets over your
bone-like algebra, your knife-still.
Any yellow your skin soaks up
from the overheads is more pleasing
than that transparent was. Here,
tug at a loose, seraphic scarf.
Tug it again. Dangle.

Landscape Drunk with You

Ginkos rattle their cups at you
on the point of the hill
where the pavement drops sharp
to imperceptible, carries
down with it your devotion
to mutable ground. This is the fact
of plumage, plummet
and counter-flight, strings pulled
through the bed you moved in.
Dawn cries of starlings punch and tug the air
until it's thick with embroidery.
"Out and under out and under out and under."
Where does it come from,
this throw of unlikeness? Each step
grows plush and frank, a leisurely
fury. The beginnings
of grass threaded by the ends
into a movable earth—which makes you
primer ink, ever-present, ever-lost.
Who called you back to canvas
and more private absorptions? The body
you leave behind is wrapped
in slippery musculature. Gaps in the
sinewy weave loose you into place.

The End Is Something None Expect

The end is something none expect in any material sense, but it came yesterday. Some contained trace of it on the floor of my apartment: small, white, warm but hard at the center where you'd expect it to be soft. Slipped it into a paper bag, down the elevator shaft and then spirited off in the trunk of my car. It had appeared there, I should say, under my couch in the city, since there'd been no place to come "from" nor go "to." It existed. Held shape. It's not my realm, but it is the means by which I escape from time to time. Why recoil? You've pressed your own mouth to the body set in place, once, and then again, below grade, graceless in our period style. Its eyes are coffee beans. The shovel makes wet kisses among pachysandra.

The Piers' (My Observers)

The piers cannot contain their own stench, all halting fullness
                              the nose plants itself in. Let us,
awkward self-gawkers, out.
                                        Mooning over the water, you
choose yourself for the prize, Tom Thompson,
                    for a higher-up, a flighty buzzing neon.

The pier likes to watch,
                    looking for a theme. Memes of "me"
multiply on its sleeve even
                    as fleshy bits stick like fresh dough
underneath and out of sight. Hooks gag,
                    smiling in place, tingling braces
                    decorative, rustic,
votive at the sea-some
                              that skirts us, flocks
to the pier. The action ratchets rocks
down to salt,   rocks that ratchet a body
                              down, naked as plankton,
                    that gooey a lucidity.

The wood rattles at your feet, suckling boy,
sugary, eating itself, digit by digit.
Ones and zeroes. Piers and oceans.
Glances, wash-a-ways.
The near-distance
          stripped to fog.

Something to stumble through, yellowing like paper.

Crowds Surround Us

The crowd surrounds us with its hands up.
An armada of embarkations and retreats,

agile founderings and piecemeal flotations.
The crowd constitutes a gravitational field

that slaps back at the ground, numbed
and maddened by ground's constant suckling.

The crowd embodies a depression in fabric
more than an attraction. Its angled, arteried, fleet

fantasias of need sway in
a loopy, bobbing dance without strings.

It's this sense of movement the organism uses
to believe in its own existence, the palpable presence

of an intangible parade, uncertain
planetary marches, a supernumerary of stars.

In its mania for artifice the crowd has sewn the sky
with these shiny extras. Embodied

adoration, they snap the organism shut
before tickling it open again

with reedy gestures. Breathe.
The crowd's louche body

clings and parts in place, an ovation

rigid and adrift, alive. It is the sea

that sweeps the sea.
Broom tight with inner bickering.

A mortal scour. Meaning,
how the crowd hates the crowd.

Outwardly. It admits you or me
as an enormous lidless eye admits glittering

beams. Endless watching, washing us in.
The crowd's object, its point,

is always vanishing into its own mass. It is a sea
with no concern for us, even as it scores.

You and Me

Today's purple hedges part their hairs on the side.
      Today's little bit can't stop smiling, except about the eyes.
My observer, my personal psychotic
      in stretched blue sweater and tight jeans
resembles you, dear, in his feel for gravity,
      that sway about the memorial fountain,
catching spray off the top statue's sternest bucket.

Destiny is an excuse for existence. And this poem
      is an excuse to pause on my way to work.
The crowd at my hip, the grass at my heels. Each person
      is an experience for others—whence vomiting.
Whence gravel and stone. Whence colic. Each person is concrete
      as in the ground—as in the gazes I've met,
her's and her's and her's again, are meeting mine.

So open, I note how different a look desire's is,
      where eyes narrow to concentrate light
on spittle and ankle, on yours and mine.
      Every metamorphosis is a glance embodied,
a history of time regained by chance.
      At the fountain two figures talk for good
in a frieze of selfless solitude, of secret.

How sentimental to record an object
      in terms of dreams and other visual experiments.
Move the object, move the sense. The world,
      wanting to be deceived, hands us looted images we tie
with great delicacy to this city, its perpetual creation
      ex-memoriam. Below us, two fast trains
rattle at their nearness, pulled nearly

off track by each other. How sentimental. How one's angle
      meets one's resistance.
One is descending, propelled, and one is reflex.
      No accurate adjustment between spirit and organ.
The individual is always dying into form.
      And Nature, a history of such things,
is a discipline of the understanding. Whence the tail's

expansion in the automated courtship of birds. And personality,
circling. Feeling for its dorm.

Recent Titles from Alice James Books

Alice James Books has been publishing exclusively poetry since 1973. One of the few presses in the country that is run collectively, the cooperative selects manuscripts for publication through both regional and national annual competitions. New regional authors become active members of the cooperative, participating in the editorial decisions of the press. The press, which historically has placed an emphasis on publishing women poets, was named for Alice James, sister of William and Henry, whose fine journal and gift for writing went unrecognized within her lifetime.

Typeset and Designed by Dede Cummings
Printed by Thomson-Shore